BOA
EDITIONS LTD

How to be Better by Being Worse

⋅⋅⋅✦⋅⋅⋅

Winner, 2019 A. Poulin, Jr. Poetry Prize

Selected by Richard Blanco

How to Be Better by Being Worse

POEMS BY

Justin Jannise

FOREWORD BY RICHARD BLANCO

A. POULIN, JR. NEW POETS OF AMERICA SERIES, NO. 45

BOA EDITIONS, LTD. ❖ ROCHESTER, NY ❖ 2021

First Edition
21 22 23 24 7 6 5 4 3 2 1

For information about permission to reuse any material from this book, please contact
The Permissions Company at www.permissionscompany.com or e-mail permdude@
gmail.com.

Publications by BOA Editions, Ltd.—a not-for-profit corporation under
section 501 (c) (3) of the United States Internal Revenue Code—are made
possible with funds from a variety of sources, including public funds from
the Literature Program of the National Endowment for the Arts; the New
York State Council on the Arts, a state agency; and the County of Monroe,
NY. Private funding sources include the Max and Marian Farash Charitable
Foundation; the Mary S. Mulligan Charitable Trust; the Rochester Area
Community Foundation; the Ames-Amzalak Memorial Trust in memory
of Henry Ames, Semon Amzalak, and Dan Amzalak; the LGBT Fund of
Greater Rochester; and contributions from many individuals nationwide. See Colophon
on page 88 for special individual acknowledgments.

Cover Design: Daphne Morrissey
Cover Art: Alice Tippit
Interior Design and Composition: Richard Foerster
BOA Logo: Mirko

BOA Editions books are available electronically through BookShare, an online distributor
offering Large-Print, Braille, Multimedia Audio Book, and Dyslexic formats, as well as
through e-readers that feature text to speech capabilities.

Library of Congress Cataloging-in-Publication Data

Names: Jannise, Justin, author. | Blanco, Richard, 1968- writer of foreword.
Title: How to be better by being worse / poems by Justin Jannise ; foreword by Richard Blanco.
Description: First edition. | Rochester, NY : BOA Editions, Ltd., 2021. | Series: A. Poulin, Jr.
   new poets of America series ; no. 45 | Summary: "Jannise's Poulin Prize-winning debut poetry
   collection subverts the self-help genre to celebrate drag culture, queer identity, and breaking
   the rules"— Provided by publisher.
Identifiers: LCCN 2020044398 (print) | LCCN 2020044399 (ebook) | ISBN
   9781950774234 (paperback) | ISBN 9781950774241 (ebook)
Subjects: LCGFT: Poetry.
Classification: LCC PS3610.A577 H69 2021 (print) | LCC PS3610.A577 (ebook) | DDC 811/.6—dc23
LC record available at https://lccn.loc.gov/2020044398
LC ebook record available at https://lccn.loc.gov/2020044399

BOA Editions, Ltd.
250 North Goodman Street, Suite 306
Rochester, NY 14607
www.boaeditions.org
A. Poulin, Jr., Founder (1938–1996)

When I'm good, I'm very good, but when I'm bad, I'm better.

Mae West

for family

Contents

Foreword

There's an abundance of *good* poetry being written today. Poetry that exhibits *good* style, exercises *good* technique, and evokes *good* sentiments. But Jannise has done more than write just another *good* book of poetry—he's written a *great* book, and beyond that, quite a *memorable* one. Why?

In a word: *Voice.* Upon simply reading the title of his first poem, "What I'm Into," it was as if Justin (not Mr. Jannise) suddenly stepped into my living room for a private poetry reading, as if I could put his book down on my lap to look up and listen to him at the mic declaiming exactly what he's *into*: "Adam's apples, beards, brains. / A certain type of man you see on trains . . ."

Voice. Not distorted by contorted syntax, not muffled by fussy semantics and obscure allusions, not muted by precious and pretentious imagery. Instead, Justin expertly commands the techniques of his craft to summon up an authentic and undeniable voice that lifts off the page, fills the room, and lets us hear him as ourselves in himself with all the varied emotional tenors and complexities of the human condition.

Voice. At times riding in on a gust of wind that suddenly bursts the front door open and blasts truth across our ears, "Get back on with your most / regrettable self. Someone / will love you." Voice. Other times carried by a breeze that caresses us for a moment, then moves on, "Let dust do / what dust does with no opinion . . ."

Voice. As comfortable as a life-long friend who's not ashamed to laugh at himself right in front of us, "I'd do better a second time around, I like / to think, but who am I kidding?" Who treats us to the humor of what we love, ". . . I love the lip sync queen // who tears her wig off during Whitney's chorus / only to reveal, you guessed it, another wig." Who's as witty as he is forthright, like Oscar Wilde's best one-liners that dare to say what we only dare to think, ". . . I prefer glamour to beauty, / the former requiring taste and the latter nothing / except sufficiently dull surroundings."

Voice. All of a sudden proverbial, "You never know what a wise man sees / unless you are a wise man." Then suddenly vulnerable with whispers of pain, "I saw no point // in saving anything for tomorrow." Then suddenly mended and empowered, ". . . but I'm freshly in love again / with the world that made me." Voice. At times wanting to speak only to the silence between lines, "These past few weeks, I've tried / to say what you may never hear."

Voice. By definition: *through the mouth; sounds distinctive to one person; conveying impressions to the mind; the right to present and receive consideration of one's desires; declare; proclaim; agency through which something is revealed.* Adding to these definitions, Justin defines voice as that which reverberates through your body, that which echoes through your psyche, that which your soul will always recall, or as Flaubert put it, that longing ". . . to make music that will melt the stars."

—Richard Blanco

PART ONE

What I'm Into

Adam's apples, beards, brains.
A certain type of man you see on trains
between Connecticut and New York:
solid muscle, a starched white shirt.

Dilfs. Doctors. Dimples. Every man I've seen
offer his arm to someone crossing the street.
Fags—those who've reclaimed the word
with piercings, tattoos, unruly curls

sprouting from their heads, pits, chests, thighs.
Ghosts of long dead poets, the sad eyes
of young Robert (Frost, Hayden, Lowell)
appearing, now, beneath the charcoal

brow of the barista. Men who make coffee, hummus, bread.
The weight of a body on the edge of the bed.
Megawatt smiles, goldspinning hips.
Intellectuals, lifeguards, motorcyclists with ripped

jeans, flabby abs, a bone to pick with the capitalist
regime. No mansplainers. No racists.
Nobody already romantically attached.
Anyone reading who thinks there's a chance.

"Until then, I'm stuck with the person that I am."

—a friend

I'm stuck with your teeth, including
the one you chipped on a fork
at the Olive Garden, surrounded by
cheerleaders, and the molar that's
still sensitive to cold after an $800 root canal
paid out of pocket.
I'm stuck with your lack of wisdom,
with your clammy hands
and allergy to penicillin.
I'm attached to your addictions.
I crave what you crave and must undertake
the task of denying it to you, at times,
for our mutual benefit.
I have no discipline when it comes
to loving your family. Even if we broke up,
I would still be friends with them.
They're so wildly talkative I can see why
you believed them when they said
you were adopted.
I'm glued to your long showers
and emergency travel plans, your tendency
to disappear without warning or explanation.
You are careless with goodbyes:
either blurting or dragging them out.
I'm married to your belly fat and hairy ass.
I own a share
of your ability to know things first.
Women who are secretly pregnant,
men hiding their affairs.
I am tied to your impatience with small talk,
your road rage, your ugly tattoos.
I am in quicksand with your death wish
as well as your knack for self-preservation.

I am pinned, like a butterfly collection,
to the blue velvet of your stubbornness.
I am as dear to you as a button
but baffled by how infrequently
you tell me this. I am crazy about
your inner gorilla, your outer flamingo.
Every day you find some new way
to smite me. The Venus flytrap does not know
it eats flies, which leads me to wonder
how much the fly knows about its manner
of death. How large does a brain have to be
to be capable of denial?
Mornings I lie awake for hours
before I can move. I've automated
the clock to brief me on the latest
travesties, preferring global discord
to the doves' nonstop coos, as I wrestle
with what makes me this way:
cocooned in living so close to work
it's too easy to make it there by 9.
Today it took listening to the same report
at 5, 6, 7, and 8 before I could rise
like Dracula in his nightgown
and hustle through my preparations.
I've been tempted to call the station.
More variety, please.

Flamingosexual

Suddenly
aware of two
pink   bruises
blooming on both   knees,
I vaguely recall
the way
I threw
myself
into bed:
back of
the hand
angled at
my temple,
a countess'
swoon. I arise
to find   my neck's out of
  whack (too many pillows), but I'm freshly in love again
 with the world that made me. Part candy, part fowl,
two-thirds feathered boa, I am not your lawn ornament.
 I am the whole lawn or nothing: St. Augustine with patches
of fine fescue. I have shrimp for breakfast, shrimp for lunch.
I skip dinner to write letters
with feathers   dipped in
       the rosy   blood
         of my   enemies,
           those who   told me
            nobody was ready for a
                 breed
                 like
                 mine.
                 But
                 I'm
                 still
                 stand-
                 ing
                 and
                 will
                 until
                 I can't.
                 I like to
                 think we
                 all carry
            within us enough fuel
         for one last blaze of renunciation.

How to Be Better by Being Worse

Ban soap. Banish suds.
Sweep the dormitory clean
of polish. Let dust do
what dust does with no opinion

from feathers.
Invite musk. Be clothed
in scandal. Smear
and smudge and slander yourself

courageous. Fuck
courage. Stick your finger
in its wet mouth and kiss
its salty neck. Slip in

as many chicken-shit deeds
as any deadbeat Dad
ever did. Forget
birthdays. Ruin Christmas.

Run people over
in conversation. Let them finish
not one sentence.
Let them sit with their own nonsense

for a second. Leave them
tongue-tied and pent up
with unexpressed vexation.
Get off the pleasant train to nowhere.

Get back on with your most
regrettable self. Someone
will love you. Someone will still fall
madly in front of you.

Falling as Adele

I was skeptical at first. It was Halloween, and I went, in drag, as Adele. I took one pill when my costume was complete and another in the Lyft on the way to the bar. By the time I got to The Eagle, let's just say I was rolling . . . in the deep. Dancing never felt so good. Thor bought me a vodka soda so I planted a lipstick kiss on his cheek. A zombie ninja grinded on me from behind. I ran my press-on nails along a Spartan's six pack. I kept losing my friends. Out of the bar's shadows, Grant emerged. Tall with a scruffy half-beard. No costume, just jeans and a loose button-down exposing a healthy bed of chest hair. A weakness of mine. He kept telling me how beautiful I was. I looked around for my friends. He was gentle, gentlemanly, a smooth talker, but hadn't I spotted him earlier, dancing with a slutty nun? "Where's your slutty nun?" I asked. He said he came alone. He bought me more vodka sodas and helped satisfy my craving for cigarettes. We danced, sweetly, my forehead nudging the crook of his jaw, his hands finding a place to rest on my hips. "Let's find your friends," he said, and when we found them, they didn't ask questions. The bar closed and we went to another. Grant bought everybody beer. He also slipped dollars into a digital slot machine until he hit the jackpot. Later, I would realize that I brought home more money than I'd left with. Where were we? Where were we headed? On the way out of the bar, I stumbled, fell in slow motion, and scraped my knee. "Nobody saw that, girl, don't worry," said Cher circa 1988, on her way in. Grant was right behind me, though he was unable—or unwilling—to stop me from hitting the ground.

Wigs Everywhere

The brown squirrel, coiled & clinging
to the guardrail of my balcony,
is a wig.

I stepped out of the shower to dry my feet
on a damp wig.

You can fold a wig in a certain way
that it becomes a cup from which you can swig

water or juice or wigskey,
which is whiskey distilled
from fermented wigs.

I met Dolly Parton & she was all wig.

Kristen Wiig is a wig.
So was Ludwig van Beethoven.

In Britain, there used to be two political parties
—the Whigs & the Wigs.

There are wigs that are mops
& wigs that seduce cops.

In some countries, it is illegal for wigs
to marry other wigs.

Have you ever slept in a wig? It's itchy.

The best wigs in life are free,
but the second-best cost
extraordinary amounts of money.

Somewhere in Detroit, you can trade
20 small wigs for one giant wig

& the award for Best Wig Ever goes to
Medusa. I love how she'd rather lose her head
than part with it

& how, even without a heart,
the head maintains its awful power.

Self-Pity

"These poems suggest a speaker wrapped in self-pity, and it's unclear if he's joking about it or perhaps half-joking to veil underlying seriousness."
—Magazine rejection slip

As carefully as we mine the caverns and grottoes of another person,
as thoroughly as we search for glints of promise, hints of betrayal,
as delicately as we manage, wanting nothing more than to live under
    the stars in peace, peace distilled from the labors of the mind,
as attentive as we are to stars, looking past the moon, forgetting it,
    wanting irrationally to be closer to what we cannot touch,
as often as we have wondered what it feels like to be struck by
    lightning, to be demagnetized, to have our currents reversed,
    to live with a new arrangement of risk and reward, to forget
    everything, everyone, to run away, to start over,
due to the truths that we have spoken despite discomfort,
due to the falsehoods we have allowed our friends to believe, careful
    not to disturb their happiness,
even when their happiness hangs like gossamer between two pillars it
    would be so cruel and so easy to knock down,
as we touch another person we have gone a long time without seeing,
    as we put a chin on his shoulder,
as sheepishly as we behave with one another, even with those we
    know best, love best,
as if we were but passengers on a small jittery plane, seatmates forced
    into the tiniest interruptions of one another's comfort, one
    another's privacy, ambitions, shame,
as if we were a tree growing next to a sidewalk, our large thick roots
    every day growing more annoying, ruining the fine linear
    path of the sidewalk, rendering it impassable,
as we put our hands into one another's hands, as we lay aside
    whatever else we might've done with them—the drumming
    or the fidgeting, the stirring or the typing—and use them
    to mean, "I'm here, I'm here with you," and use them to say,
    "I'm stupid and I'm lost and I have none of the answers you're
    looking for,"

as uselessly as we try to comfort the grieving,
as pointlessly as we try to reason with the idiotic,
as foolishly and greedily as we luxuriate in doing the right thing,
      in having answered when called, in having helped when
      summoned,
and for never having received this charity back, not in equal measure,
      not precisely, not like we thought we would,
      we take pity on ourselves.

Let Me Eat Cake

I'm having a reproductive day, biting off more than I can glue. Children approach me. One wants to attach a plastic ruby to her shoe. Another wants help building a robot out of paper cups. My fingers throb with blisters. A girl smashes a mirror with her fist, demands I glue it back. Each fragment glitters with an essay, a voice commanding me to reflect. But while it is natural it is by no means necessary the way one word out of place can ruin a baby, how badly I want to drown my sorrows with drink. How I still want to be, I don't know, useful. My mother wouldn't let me do much in the kitchen. I was told to watch the biscuits. I watched them burn.

Stingray Petting Zoo

I never would have guessed they were so pushy,
shoving each other at the edges of their tank

as if our outstretched, soap-washed hands
could turn them over to face the stars.

I think I saw one smirk before it splashed me
with a magician's well-rehearsed sleight of

fin? wing? cape? What is the world
hiding with its moon-dark flank

and ciliated underbelly? Now, white-knuckled
in weekend traffic, I grip the wheel

with the same fingertips that caressed the creature's
slippery-slick bone because—how can I explain this?—

it dismissed my fear and intimated a choice:

    Come, be stung by the wildness of life, or else

    go on standing there in the plunging temperatures
    of the cold shoulder you turn

    to what you think you understand
    —most of all, yourself

    as you were moments ago, in the glass tunnel
    where the sharks bare their glassy teeth.

I've been known to circle the block,
having failed to recognize

the climbing ivy, shutters, and terracotta shingles
of my own house.

Must I pay dearly
for my lack of planning? I watch

hours of traffic sink like sediment
and harden into bedrock.

Bladder full, I squirm and curse and try to catch
the eye of anyone who'll make room for my

immediate exit. A truck driver nearly assists
but I plant my foot on the break instead

and another window passes me by.
Sigh. It's no use.

I belong miles below, and miles behind
the overnight world. Overnight, yes—

it is in this way, I am told,
I cannot be expected to change.

PART TWO

Leather Jacket

Copper-brown and sueded,
with a fleece lining and Western collar,
It's so heavy, my mother says,
picking it up at the shoulders
and giving it a weak shake
that releases a speck of lint.
Heavy is her word for expensive,
and she seems proud and comforted
that I walk around feeling warm and important.

How much? My father speaks up
—my father, who, every winter of his life
has worked outside in a Carhartt knockoff.
He examines the label,
hand-sewn in golden thread,
and the sturdy buttons,
of which only one is missing.
He wants to hear me admit how I overpaid,
—the folly of it.

So I tell them the story.
Vintage thrift store, mid-July.
I take two jackets to the dressing room,
similar in style
but one is clearly made of heavier substance,
and noticing a $30 difference,
I switch the price tags.
The girl at the counter actually says, *What a steal.*

Now, if you're expecting my parents
to groan with disapproval,
or to make some appeal
to the eighth commandment,
then I should tell you that all their lives
they've been robbed.

At the End of a Long Stay at the Manor of the Absurd

I leave behind a lot of empty wine bottles.
You said eat anything in the fridge and I did
right down to the last gherkin.
Unrelated: your turtle is dead.
You failed to mention it and I failed
to notice it in time. I know more about you
than I ever wanted. A note in the cabinet reads
If you want your marriage to succeed,
then you have to learn to forgive.
Things I don't let dogs do:
lick me, lean on me, initiate touch.
I constantly back away from them,
locking them in or out while I eat cereal
or smoke one of your cigars on the patio.
I hold my nose when I pet them,
teaching them that some hearts are rotten
and full of contempt. When my niece
grew tall enough to ride every carnival ride, I said
Congrats, now you're an extra twelve dollars.
It rained yesterday and I let the dogs
run through the mud. It never occurred to me
to clean them before letting them in.
I made more money working the drive-thru
at a burger chain that has since burned down.
Not the whole chain just the one I worked at.
Your neighbor told me that houses
in this part of town get burglarized.
I'll start locking the door when I leave.
Your dogs chewed up a throw pillow.
You may want to empty that vacuum
before using it. I've been staying on top of
your mail. So far, nothing worth keeping.

I'm taking back the giraffe soap dispenser I bought on Black Friday

Turns out I already had one.
And the hundred-year-old seed
my great-grandmother passed down
that I can't do anything with—I'm going to ruin it
in a tumbler of water on my nightstand.
I shouldn't have been so bitchy
to the optometrist, but he dug those frames
into my temples and planted that pressure
in my skull. What's the difference
between a buzzard and a duck?
Family. What's the difference between a family
and a brood? Nothing. The father
abandons both. Shame that
the German genitive is dying,
that *The Wizard of Oz* was not intended
for screens as small as televisions,
that walrus meat ferments in a bag of skin.
I'll stop complaining about waiting in line.
"Nude Grandparents" has no business as a title.
"Innuendo" does. . . . Maybe. I don't know
where I get off apologizing for
conducting my education in public.
What public? Tell me the difference again
between a bivouac and a campsite. I love hearing
each word used to bring the other down.

That time my aunt stole a Stetson from a dead dentist

It didn't fit. She couldn't return it. Crickets.
We went in for a night cap, and she said she hated her mother
for dying and leaving her here, in Panama,
and making her swear to finish this damn campaign.
She withdrew a Xanax from her pillbox
and retired to her boudoir, drink in hand.
Alone, I let my thoughts return to the lifeguard, whose only job
for hours was to watch me, the beach being otherwise deserted.
I made a halfhearted attempt at drowning, but under his visor
he remained stone still. Rude. My inner gambler suggested
chatting him up to see if he knew of a party.
That's when a family of four arrived with their huge umbrella
and I knew I would never escape. Should've been a trucker.
Boss of the plains tearing my rig across the open road.
Fifty-cent showers and pork pies flaky under golden lamps.
Dropping gifts from coast to coast, like Santa, only
less creep, more pith. Moths splattered on the windshield, fat as birds.

House-sitting for a month puts tires on my Toyota

So I can steer past the dog carcass drawing flies
like last night's drunks
unleashed to the boulevard.
Pay to park. Swill a couple hand grenades and why not
spend a night in jail, sleep it off?
I prefer a silver cage with four-wheel drive
and the airports and cities
it laces in tighter. Once off the ground
I'm timing my own high jump, waiting
to land. Slow-cam on the
jelly glob hanging dearly to its spoon.
Open wide. Here comes the
crack of thunder, the free-fall, the fruit
smack splattering over news channels
as the walls back politely away.
Pointless how some midair visions land safely
while others avoid carrying on.
I can take or leave
the coffers filling up with esteem
as long as I maintain a certain number of cars
circling the roundabout. Distraction yields
to the city's self-indulgence overtaken,
as it were, by a need for peace. There is no
shopping for peace,
only standing in line as if for bread
expecting a somewhat sufficient portion.
Here comes the bill
for the black tie with cummerbund
that matches those of the cousins and high school bandmates
who, if the bride were found stuffed between
panels of Sheetrock, no one would think
to question. Can I be bought so cheaply?
I owe a friend a visit.
I owe homage to the damp night air.

I fall victim to my own refunding
as a ball juggled poorly falls,
bounces, rolls uphill and stops
beneath a wing-tipped loafer.
Stiff pant-leg. Gold cufflinks. Watch.
How much lower can I lower myself?
I owe another stranger what he wants.

Ways to Do It

After dinner or
Arrested, in handcuffs
In an Applebee's Parking Lot
Above a baseball diamond
Addled out across from a Denny's or
Before breakfast, between shifts, beyond reason
Bent over a sawhorse
Bareback, reverse cowgirl
Cream-pied, coked-out threesome in a timeshare
Daddy's dirty little egret spreading her tail feathers
In drag, in Delaware, in Denmark, inverted Diplomat
Eiffel tower effigy
In a stranger's car, the smell of stale French fries
Geraniums hanging off the mantle, exposed brick
India. Arie humming in the background
Interlaced with iPhone charger, alarm
Jet-lagged, hairy-legged, Krispy Kreme-pied or
Longingly attached, marsupial, fetal
Like rabbits
Missionary
Outdoors at 3 a.m., on Molly, on meth, at a park
Over and over and over
Past sunrise
Poised, dignified
Puffing purple punch
Quietly—silently, so as not to be heard
Stilettoed, stockinged, strangled
Swooning, quaking while the repairman buries his face
Under your skirt
Tentacled—brainily clinging
Undercover, under the influence, upside-down bank robber
Valiantly, knowing this is it, this is where you kiss it
An extra time, for the memories
With horns locked, with minty fresh breath

Without air-conditioning
While falling, while choking, while crying
While begging you not to stop
You on top, me as far south
As New Zealand

More than just on sleeves, the heart is worn

on wedding gowns, caps-and-gowns and backless
hospitals. It skis across hardwood floors
in dirty-soled pantyhose pulled down to the knee.
Couched in tied-together shoes, it flings itself
over a telephone wire and hangs, listening in.
There is no heart, then. There are bunny slippers,
burqas, trenches and bracelets, both slap and slave.
There is the peignoir and the tagelmust,
the steel-toe boots my father wore,
cotton smock-frocks, hand-smeared aprons, nightshirts,
loincloths and skeleton suits washed to rags
and threads like those of conversations we have
with no one in particular on trains.

Passengers, 1938

As I was saying about poinsettias,
they belong on a hat as much as a shoe
belongs on the tail of my fur coat.
Remove them both, please—
I detest a muddied hem.

I'm only saying that because
there'll be no one there to greet us
when this train finally arrives.

      If it ever does.
Whose finger-painted husband
designed this schedule, anyway? I haven't any
need for company that earns its living
hawking electricity
at the expense of pleasing, natural vistas.

At least we both know that emeralds
have exhausted themselves
on the masses.

      I'll not argue there.
Our differences frolic in the shade
our respective fortunes provide.
Avant-garde—I dismiss any harlot
who dares utter the phrase. On what
earth would she not be a lithograph
of a woman undertaking her own handsomeness
too late?

      I am one to talk with all the spare parts
that keep this engine running.
The conductor owes me a favor—
shall I spend it on a stop at the dairy farm?
I've heard tell of the ingenuity

of dairy farmers when it comes to machines.
They must have some contraption
to stop one from making that face.

Indeed, my face is quite in need of a break
from what twists it into this horror,
though I doubt flirtation with the conductor
will change it much. Perhaps I ought to beg him
for a mule that won't bray at one's
gentlemanly fists.

Funny I should mention mules,
when I was just wondering why they
always seem to fall dead on the plow
midway between the house
and the nearest pastry. I should take
pity on the poor creatures
and invest in a bus pass. I've heard
buses come equipped with entrances
designed specifically for people with an
appetite for . . . what's that they call it? Beauty?

I prefer glamour to beauty,
the former requiring taste and the latter nothing
except sufficiently dull surroundings.
Men fall in love with vineyards, never with a girl
who lives near one.

This penchant for analogy is stunning.
Am I to assume I can ward off crows
better than the eyes avert their feet?

I assume whichever posture
corrects the curve in my spine.

Was I slouching? Must be the seats.

The seats recline not.

Mascot

Never remove your head
in front of children. That's the rule.
Friendly, giant, ostracized cartoon,
overstuffed skull. Has us
shifting our weight on the benches.
Has us turning around
for the pretzel's bland dough.
Like a real animal, *evolved*.
Trended so big there, now
circling back to small.
Now wheeling along the string lights
of the sidelines. Soon catapulting,
center court, wielding cause
after reactionary cause.
Is there a skit—a duel? a draw? —afoot?
A stadium wave to throw ourselves into
by staying put?

On Piety Street, the people all are pierced

and tattooed, spilling out of the Irish pub
with green Mohawks and glittery kilts,
weeks before St. Patrick's (or is it days after?)
the blackouts blending into hangovers and back.
Tropical, seasonless weather. Perennial palms.

The town tells time by parades, by floods
of outsiders pouring in to sop their biscuits
in a runny *bontemps* yolk.
Laissez . . . roulez . . . the whole nine yielding to
cloud nine, a feeling that too much
may yet be enough. Best another spin

of the roulette wheel, another dip
into the pool where no one says no.
Oh, but all anybody talks about is how
as little as five years ago, things were just
wilder, filled with more smoke.
A troupe of Lost Boys patrolled the streets,
raccoon tails tucked between their legs.
The river coughed a body a week. No one felt safe.

Now only the young can afford to ignore
culture's expanding blandness, its milquetoast *roux*.
Gutter punks may ravish politicians' signs, but
every would-be mayor watches,
mustachioed and devil-horned,
from the corner of St. Claude,
smiles like blank-eyed sorority girls
who carry each other home.

Poem with Trap Door

Call in sick to work
and spend all day
driving the wrong way
up the interstate's tight, puckered ass.
When asked for your name, say
Flintstone. When asked for your signature,
write illegibly in red.
See how long you can go
eating only free samples.
Most gyms offer trial memberships
just to get you through the door.
I'm not telling you to lie, I'm asking,
What's the truth even for in this circus?
I hope I don't offend any hardscrabble trapeze artists
or my Facebook friends
who can be counted on
for compulsive updates about their many successes,
each slice of layered cake on a white plate
at a restaurant whose existence is the surest sign
of how far technology has advanced the dark arts.
Not that I'm *not* complicit,
the me who mainlines pour-over coffee and enjoys
a good pigeon pose.
Closing my eyes, I see a pig wearing Ruby Woo lipstick.
Maybe she's born with it,
maybe it's the same ol' same ol'
delivered now so boldly
that I am left,
like a child at a mall,
small and stunned.
Who knew it was even possible
that my mother could forget me,
abandoning me to a fate
like the cat lady's whose bones had to be found

between the walls of her Jack-and-Jill
two years after she went
missing. If you want to be euphemistic
about tragedy, describe it
the way a cloud would.
Two cars collide on the highway
and nobody gets out. Levees break
into an extended pool party.
She must be tired from pruning.
There she goes,
inside. Fewer homes
like hers nowadays.
High-rises are booming.

PART THREE

Three Self-Portraits

1. As Waves Crashing

I was told // to stop // I did not
stop // I was warned // that once
I raged against the rocks // there

would be no undoing // I was
told I would be // forgotten
I remember // the way // that word

was meant to sound // crushing
the thought like a window // left open
at night // to let the wrong thing in.

I was rash // I was washing // my hands
of the dirt // and the hurt // I'd let
collect there // I saw no point

in saving anything for tomorrow.
I crashed // and crashed // the way a
madman on the run // weaves through traffic.

Touch me // I'll shoot // I'll go
bang bang // against all I see // as yours
and not mine. You shook // your ass

and said it was // ours. Now it's dust.
Without a sea // properly
to seethe against // still // I seethed.

2. With an Axe to Grind

I was rash / I was washing / my hands
of the dirt / and the hurt / I'd collected there
all the grime / from all the times / I'd wished

for you / to hold me / all the filth
from the fifty-odd instances / of
promise, broken / expectation, unmet

and like a rat whose length is 80% / tail
I dragged / myself / to the chopping / block
and waited / for the axe / to fall

I didn't want to go on / weighed down
by the me / that I'd been / carrying
just as now / I am trying / to write you

out of my mind / I'm not very good at it.

3. With a Bitter Pill to Swallow

When you loved me, I stood outside of time,
    like the chief security officer in a room
full of screens monitoring my past and future.

Footage of me gorging on melt-in-the-mouth
    mounds of chocolate lava cake, a shower
of sparks. Footage of you and me forging ahead

in the roomy cab of your Ram, hands held,
    the dust of our menthols blowing around.
And because I was loved, I felt free to ask,

What about buttons? boxes? paper fans?
    Is there closure only in what we make?
Dolls, doors, arguments.

A smoking jacket, a purse.
    Let there be closure on the subject
of closure. That it is false, like a golden calf.

That it is wrong, like a hand brought hard
    against a face. These past few weeks, I've tried
to say what you may never hear.

You're no good for me anymore.
    And I want you back.

An Extra Heart

I wish I were as fabulous as Titus
removing a pair of sunglasses

in one swift and open-mouthed swoop
only to reveal another pair

beneath the first. The drama, the preparation,
that pixelated shoulder-wiggle

he throws in for added effect—I love it
as much as I love the lip sync queen

who tears her wig off during Whitney's chorus
only to reveal, you guessed it, another wig.

Something about the way she understands
the gesture of taking our expectations

and handing them back to us, foiled, doubled.
Dinner is served, Madame. Please find

another covered dish. Take the elevator to the second
elevator. Open the door to the door.

I wish I'd had a plan for all the times
a man caught me off guard. If I'd known

he was suddenly going to say he needed space
I might've thought to bring

an extra heart. Here is what you've broken.
Keep it. One will do me.

And wouldn't I give anything to go back
and tell my father that during those difficult years

I felt safer when he was around? And when he tries,
as he always did, to buy my love with money,

I'll hand my love over to him, easily, as I never did.
And I'll keep some for myself, as I never could.

Claire's Husband

I never had to worry about getting caught.

If I said I was at the gym, that's probably where I was.

Emerson, on denying handouts to beggars: "Are these *my* poor?"

A deep, doggish sadness in their eyes.

I remember the first time I knew the man's wife.

She'd made some interesting leaps across the country.

Wedding bands, work schedules, five o'clock shadows rough against my cheek.

I allowed myself to be turned on by the very things that were supposed to deter me.

My job was to edit profiles for the department website.

Are these my vows? *My* unfaithful?

Claire's was the only one that came to me with clean style, perfect grammar.

I, too, was chained to that fence.

Claire's husband was ruggedly put together.

We met maybe three or four times, on Sundays, when she believed he was on the river, waking up his body.

He talked about her a lot, actually. They often did.

When I said I needed more, I meant coffee

but we were midway through "real talk"
and, logically, I might have been responding
to your desire to see less of me.
The dark film developing at the base
of my mug was taking me back to Kansas,
a clapboard bed-and-breakfast, the streets
that day or night were dead empty.
Between the two of us, we had enough
to live there for a month.
How many dime-store novels do you think
we could have read aloud to each other
in that floral-patterned room, between meals
and lying down as long as we could stand it,
wrapped up in ourselves like the damp towels
we let fall to the floor?

Bohemian Rhapsody at the Cat Café

Dearly beloved, we assemble here
today to mourn "dating."
I've already gone on twelve
this year and it's barely May.
Honeysuckle and night-blooming jessamine
emit a perfume slutty with
renewal, and yet my Public Library branch
e-mails, calling *Heart of Darkness*
back unread. Now

I may never know how Conradian
this journey will become.
So far its peg fits squarely
into the Theater of the
Absurd's round hole, deck chairs and ottomans brought
inside to furnish a makeshift
scene of repose in front of Freddie Mercury's
overhyped biopic, while cats
(I count 30)

mew, hiss, play, splay, swat, nuzzle, and swing from
chandeliers like coked-out
hair band guitarists trapped in
some midsize city's Hilton.
My beau for the evening, Nathaniel (I swiped right
while swooning over a long-haired
Persian in his profile photo) comes here "a lot"
and doesn't know he bears my ex's,
Shane's, middle name.

I guess I'm what you'd call a fair weather
feline friend—admirer,
really. Occasional fan.
I used to pet the courtyard

tabby until I caught it digging up my
outdoor plants. Nathaniel suggested the movie
but it was optimism that
blinded me when

I anticipated more emphasis
on café, less on cat:
leather sofas, magazine
racks, smooth Indie rock, the whirr
and bang of an espresso maker, the smell of
roasted beans, students, retirees,
tattooed musicians cutting tracks on their laptops
—maybe a fluffy one or two
afoot, asleep.

What I get is fur flying, odors foul
and frisky, Folger's black,
Nathaniel—even if
he'd been Shane's twin he'd never
have escaped the womb intact—a wounded soul,
poor boy, innocent, jittery,
and a lazy conversationalist. Besides,
the movie traps me in what I've
tried to avoid:

my lonely thoughts, how love is fantasy,
caught in a landslide, no
escape from reality.
And nothing Rami Malek
mouths or belts can neutralize my wish to flee.
With apologies to Nathaniel,
I get my wish.

He stays behind, preferring his furry
company ("cabbages
to men," as in Woolf's *To the Lighthouse*)
while *Shane* Nathaniel gravel

crunches under my tires—he liked dogs, but he
favored me. What split us up? I
want to take an arrow from my quiver of blame
and aim it at Shane's cavalier,
too-cool-for-school

approach to my "needs," as I called them when
he said he'd be home late
and never showed. I needed
him to close the gap I saw
widening between his actions and his words.
I needed his cock in my mouth
to stop me from yammering about how scary
it was to love someone so much
so fast, as if

our togetherness were becoming both
the basin and the drain,
both the bill and its veto,
the word *yes* and the letter *(wh)y?*
I'd do better a second time around, I like
to think, but who am I kidding?
One bad script, a couple dozen ugly kitties
and I'm out the door. Mama, oh
I'm miles away.

Mercury in Retrograde

And there was that time I came home to find him
     washing the sheets,

and there was that night he went to his buddy's
     but he trimmed his ruddy beard first,

and at that gallery opening, when he rushed me
     through the sculptures, eying a girl who'd just walked in,

and there were those times I had to remind myself
     to trust.

How now it seems like a cigarette lit onstage,
     the firecracker smell and the smoke.

Such are the effects and such are the scenes:
     fear of getting close; dinner, the arrangement of.

And then the negligence of those arrangements,
     the lack of all things commitment, of all things, respect.

Only with a smattering of sunlight, only
     under a patch of blue paper,

only until you've gone so long without touch
     will he gently touch you

not with any force, but with some insistence,
     from behind, on your shoulder, on your neck.

And it is some relief to know he's there,
     and it is some relief to weep.

Splitsville

It was no fault of mine
that Friday night turned
into a waste bin,
bagless and full of mango peel,
nine gnawed chicken bones
and Coke bottles empty but for lime wedges
stuffed past their long throats
and into their souring bellies
which give clues about how far away
we are
but none that explain whether I left
because of you
or because I wanted to leave
and waited for you to become the reason.

The Sublime

I want to punch the mountains
in the face, he says,
How dare they be so gorgeous!
His beard glows red.

The only other man I've known
who's said these words:
my father, young, shaking his fist
at hummingbirds.

What does it say about them?
What does it say of me?
They'd rather ruin what they love,
and I'm their company.

(for S.N.G.)

PART FOUR

I'm writing well for no one but myself

I drop a period
where it belongs and you
would rather me not because
you've seen that done before
and certain memories yield
a certain urge to nail
the ripped-up flooring to the roof.
And I want to say I get that
but I don't.

Fireflies

You, too, have stood by the window,
face scarred by moonlight,
counting the small green orbs.

Today, only four.

We have reached the point
where our souls are lifted by the glow
of a neighbor's cigarette,

even though it's the wrong color
and has no peer
in this darkness.

Little Poem Complex

After Kay Ryan and Sigmund Freud

Every little
poem loves its
mother, wants
on some other
level besides
the simple
to marry her
insider's sense of
quiet knowing
with its own bent on
overthrowing
the jealous,
distant
father—he who
possesses want
like a theory.
Just not every
poem loves so
clearly.

Bullion Depository

Deep in Kentucky, behind
twelve percent of the world's
chain links, past snipers' sights
and paperwork bundled into
granite-lined, torch-resistant, blear impenetrability,
a vault of gold!

I bet it's empty,
says my mother, channel-
surfing
extremely slowly.
She gives each niche-
driven network its due time to woo her—
a relic of a sense of trust.

Soon enough, the History Channel
cuts to a scholar-turned-
Doomsday analyst
who says, effectively,
I bet it's empty.
That he and I graduated from the same bastion of
higher learning doesn't help.

It's not empty. It can't be,
I say, dousing my mother with a theory of a theory
I've been hearing on the radio.
She believes me.
And then she flips the channel to
a sporting event: men on the beach, but not volleyball,
playing by rules
nobody understands.

After Visiting My Brother in Prison

On some level, we all want what he has:
ample time, and not to have to worry
over the tide of tasks. Today my account
dropped to negative 30, out of nowhere,
like the icy air from a freak weather pattern.
Someone in Mexico's got my pin number.
After hours spent haggling with robot voices,
I wonder if that's the real me—splurging
on department store handbags in Ixtapa.
Look at this road, intent on reminding us
of nothing but its roadness, its hard, gravelly
grayness with patches of black, gummy asphalt
and potholes. Look at this little car,
barely capable of getting us back and forth
to Huntsville, along this road, through these woods
that echo the industrial Pine Sol they splash
across the floors and key-carved counters.
Look at her—careworn, frazzled—her restlessness
interrupted solely by going to work
and getting home, where hopefully someone's thought
to put food on the table. Look at me, the likeness
of my father when he was at his most unforgivable.
Always drunk. Always angry. Always
pushing someone around on his bow-legged
journey. Poor old man, they say, to the sack
of regret he is now.
                    My brother gives me
tight hugs when I go to see him. I ought to say
go to touch him, to feel the warmth in his cheeks
and palms, to feel my bones crack beneath him.
Sometimes, when he catches me by the shoulders and pulls
me toward him, so the foreign smell behind
his ears, which must be the smell of inside,
is so close it nearly chokes me, I get the feeling

he's holding on to the brief scattering of years
that passes for childhood, like burying your head
in a tree, closing your eyes, and counting
to fifty, or a hundred—as high as it takes
for everyone around you to find a place to hide.

Minor Adjustments

My eyes are fixed on a small, dark thing,
one of many, on blue and white tile.

Concealed knowledge is buried treasure.

Blake said, A fool sees not the same tree
that a wise man sees.

Blake wrote, You never know what is enough
unless you know what is more than enough.

My eyes remain fixed on the small, dark thing
that writhes on the linoleum.

One storm, and a tree gives up all its berries.

A fool said, The storm stripped the berries
from the unprotected trees.

My eyes come into focus on the black insect,
overturned and kicking,
on the blue and white floor.

One storm, and a tree gives up.

You never know what is enough
until you have had less than enough.

The black insect, overturned and kicking
its legs, gives up momentarily.

A fool says what he thinks
the wise man sees.

You never know what a wise man sees
unless you are a wise man.

I see berries on the sidewalk.

I smell their rotting flesh.

I run over their carcasses and the sound
of them popping accrues until a dog barks.

The overturned insect is kicking only five
of its legs.

Only a fool would wish to be a woman.

Only women are wise.

One storm, one of many—
you never—no, you always
know what is enough.

You just want more berries,
more sacrifices rotting on the pavement,
more dogs barking.

The bug manages to right itself!

The bug has set itself in motion.

A fool sees a tree with an X and thinks
buried treasure.

A wise man sees a tree with an X and begins
to write an elegy for the tree that will outlive him.

One woman,
one of many you'll never know,

says you have more than enough berries
because none are needed.

The insect needs all six legs to move
and one is not moving.

The insect needs all six legs to move
and five of them are fools.

Mother and Child

At a small church far back
past the oil field and rice paddies
old hippies who'd quit dope for Jesus
kept their braids and tambourines.

Sister Jenny, with her big tinted glasses
and electric guitar, took me by the hand,
rescuing me and another boy
from the anguish of the adult sermon.

One lesson, I recall, was about Samson,
his comic book abs, his rock star hair
and the jawbone of an ass he slew Philistines with.
We agreed to say donkey, not ass.

Was it important for us boys never to mix up God
with women, never to let Delilah crash
and then move in, replacing Him in our hearts?
Or were we dealt just the facts with a coloring sheet?

Memory fades like faces in the back pew:
Silent men with yellowing mustaches
who came to hear but did not come to be saved.
I realize now how young my mother was then,

how a woman with amber eyes and a shy smile,
whose husband never showed,
would want to sit near the front
protected by the bright light of the baptismal,

by the sisters who sang and prayed over the potluck.
I can see, now, too, the innocence of the pastor's mistake,
a man so tall and gentle I think I believed
he was religion itself.

He called on my mother to lead us all in prayer.
My heart sank.

Without ever having been told, I—and I alone—
knew the mortality of this wound.
How embarrassed she would be, how stubborn.
She shook her head.
The stunned pastor called on someone else.

It might've been the first time I ever hated her,
as if she were *my* child, sucking her thumb
instead of getting us through
the moment with less pain.
In the intervening years, I've read about

battered women who come to see all men
as accomplices in their abuse.
For another person, that's the end of the story.
Still another might have known from the outset
that he wanted to put to rest once and for all

that burning sense of shame,
even though it was a tiny moment
immediately forgotten and now long past.
Another person might have forgiven and been absolved.
Another might have switched it all around:

It was the son who was asked to pray,
the son who refused.
It was the mother who that day knew she could hate him.
It was the son who remained silent,
the mother who wept into her hands.

Midnight

Who wants to die
with corn in their teeth?
I'll take the slice of pumpkin
but refuse to have it served
on a silver platter.
I have morals.
My neighbor the other day,
daubing her brush
into the small-scale ramp
of coral orange, pouting out
a wet-lip shimmer on
her front door trim—
I wanted not to warn her
cars passing could see, well
they could see her
granny panties
every time she bent.
And me? I saw the copper Chevy
in the drive at 9 a.m.
I must have heard the engine
crank, the break
release and then? By ten
I was popping Munchkins and wincing
at the folded copper heap
being sledged from the ditch,
remembering the Pomeranian
my wheels pummeled under me,
bumpety-thump. Its
heavier-than-expected, wet fur bag
of bones clung to the road as I tried
not to see my headlights
reflected in its dead eyes.
Man, things are
lifeless bodies before they turn

to carcasses and then to
something fuzzy
facing the corner.
I learned that. Preparing for the worst makes
randomness unfold
with the satisfaction of I-told-you-so.
That, I need to hear again.

The Afterlife

Here, nobody
is what you'd call
deep. Mister Vroom Vroom
cruises his Vette
around the beach.
Lady Frills
raises her pinky over tea
and gossip, porcelain hounds
dotting the mantle
of her B&B.
Bums come here
to be bums.
Nudists arrive to be free
and shyly stick
to the northwest edge,
where palm trees
are shoots
culminating
in crowns of leaves.
Sunsets are
signature orange
and indigo. Sand,
granular
and comfortable.
Here, you almost forget
your inner ear,
its labyrinth
of muscle, its
dedication
to balance.

Head in the Sand

Tempting
to cling

to some certainty,
this memory,

that fact
about peaches and not retract

in the face of certain dirt.
Possible to remain inured

to the funneling away
of fuel, the always-nearly-empty gauge,

despite such frequent sojourns
to the pump. Tough to worship the book's closure

and remain readerly.
Tougher to hug the mystery

as close to the chest as a lung,
or to know how your tongue

tastes. Tougher still
to go through with the burial

when the coast
is eroding, and the forecasts

say
rain every day.

Booked

I almost slipped   not on a banana peel
but on a banana, *peeled*. Naked.
Just the sweet, soft, easily edible part.
Lying there on the sidewalk, the inverse of a joke.
We all have days when the door
that should be unlocked won't open.
Nothing under the welcome mat
but crushed, red leaves and cockroach limbs.
Voices from the vestibule carry scraps
of a heated argument   in from the cold—
. . . *we've been through this* . . . *be honest* . . . *not surprised* . . .
I took an alternate route to work and saw
a barn with a landscape painted on its side.
I saw one, two, three bald pumpkins in a field
before the word caught up and erased them
into a patch. I skimmed a few pills from the childproof bottle
and dropped them, like glittery slivers of flint,
along my way   out.
                     I'm never going back.
My three-pronged cord wouldn't take
to the dual outlets of that house.
My friend, the masseuse,
hurries to work this morning, believing herself booked.
Her first appointment doesn't show. The second calls to cancel.
The third shows up an hour late. Apologies, apologies—
It's the strangest thing, but on his way he got rear-ended
and the crick in his neck disappeared. Like that, he snaps,
and drops a twenty into her unused hands.
As the time for her fourth appointment draws nearer,
she weighs the odds. . . .
         They lean towards rockets launching
           into the steadfast ground.

Acknowledgments

My gratitude to the following publications in which these poems originally appeared, often in altered form:

The Awl: "Mascot";
Best New Poets: "'Until then, I'm stuck with the person that I am.'";
Columbia Journal Online: "Bullion Depository" (originally "A Quarter to Midnight"), "House-sitting for a month puts tires on my Toyota" (originally "Seven Minutes to Midnight"), "Midnight";
Copper Nickel: "Leather Jacket";
Electric Literature: "Wigs Everywhere";
The Good Men Project: "After Visiting My Brother in Prison";
Hobart: "At the End of a Long Stay at the Manor of the Absurd" (originally "Dean Young");
Kestrel: "Claire's Husband," "Mother and Child";
Lana Turner: "Ways to Do It";
Malasaña Arts & Letters: "When I said I needed more, I meant coffee," "More than just on sleeves, the heart is worn";
Moon City Review: "What I'm Into";
New Haven Review: "Head in the Sand";
New Ohio Review: "How to Be Better by Being Worse";
Of Zoos: "Little Poem Complex";
Palette Poetry: "The Afterlife";
The Pinch: "Flamingosexual";
Public Poetry: "Booked";
San Antonio Express-News: "Fireflies";
The Southeast Review: "Mercury in Retrograde";
Split Lip Magazine: "An Extra Heart";
Verdad: "Minor Adjustments";
Yale Review: "Stingray Petting Zoo."

This work would not have been possible without the support and encouragement of my family and friends, teachers and classmates, fellow editors and institutional leaders, many of whom sadly are no longer with us. In alphabetical order, they are: Miah Arnold, Katharine Barthelme, Emily Barton, Tammy and Tim Beam, Erin Belieu, Beau Box, Stephanie Brown, Laura Calaway, Sally Connolly, Jennifer and Jonathan Craig, Laura H. and Dennis Damon, Chitra Divakaruni, Timothy Ellison, Emily Foxhall, Nick Flynn, James Galvin, Benjamin Garcia, Shane Guillory, Tony Hoagland, Robbie Howell, Toby Jannise, Ruby and T. J. Jannise, Richard Kenney, Christine Kwon and Cooper Lewis, Rich Levin, Mark Levine, Dora Malech, Misty Matin, J. D. McClatchy, Wayne Miller, Charlotte Pence, Krupa Parikh, Alex Parsons, Raj Persaud, D. A. Powell, Joy Priest, Kevin Prufer, Paige Quiñones, Sarah Robinson, Martha Serpas, Kaj Tanaka, Giuseppe Taurino, Roberto Tejada, Matthew Weber, Marie and Ernie Wickesser, and Michael Zilkha.

I am further indebted to the editors, designers, and staff at BOA Editions, Ltd., who took such great care making this book. Their names are Peter Conners, Ron Martin-Dent, and Daphne Morrissey. Thank you to Alice Tippit, who kindly allowed her work to be used on the cover, and to MaryScott Hagle, Lynda Le, and Miranda Ramírez, who took my author photos. A special thanks goes to poets Richard Blanco, Franny Choi, Cate Marvin, and Tomás Q. Morín, each of whom—within the span of a few months, and unbeknownst to one another—chose to recognize my work. Humbly do I recognize theirs here.

For sharing their limited time and limitless generosity, thank you to Erin Belieu and D. A. Powell. And for being my best teacher, biggest cheerleader, strongest protector, and most loyal confidante, thank you at last to my mother, Brenda K. Jannise. She raised me right.

About the Author

Justin Jannise grew up in rural southeast Texas. As a first-generation college student, he attended Yale University, where he won the 2009 Albert Stanburrough Cook Prize for Poetry. He worked as a freelance pop culture writer in New York City before moving to Iowa to attend the Iowa Writers' Workshop. The University of Iowa awarded him a Teaching-Writing Fellowship in 2013 and named him the Provost's Visiting Writer in Poetry in 2014. Now finishing his Ph.D. in Literature and Creative Writing at the University of Houston, Justin served a two-year term as Editor-in-Chief of *Gulf Coast: A Journal of Literature and Fine Arts.* He frequently teaches workshops for Inprint, Grackle & Grackle, and Writespace. As part of Writers in the Schools, he has led classrooms at Field Elementary School, the High School for Law and Justice, and M.D. Anderson Cancer Hospital. He is the recipient of both the Inprint Marion Barthelme Prize and the Inprint Verlaine Prize in Poetry. In 2019, his poems appeared in both *Best New Poets* and *Best of the Net,* and *Copper Nickel* nominated his poem "Leather Jacket" for a Pushcart Prize. His poem "Flamingosexual" won the 2020 Pinch Literary Award. His writing has also appeared—or is forthcoming—in *Hobart, Houston Chronicle, Lana Turner, New Ohio Review, Out, Palette Poetry, The Southeast Review, Split Lip Magazine,* and *Yale Review.*

BOA Editions, Ltd.
The A. Poulin, Jr. New Poets of America Series

Colophon

BOA Editions, Ltd., a not-for-profit publisher of poetry and other literary works, fosters readership and appreciation of contemporary literature. By identifying, cultivating, and publishing both new and established poets and selecting authors of unique literary talent, BOA brings high-quality literature to the public. Support for this effort comes from the sale of its publications, grant funding, and private donations.

❖

The publication of this book is made possible, in part, by the support of the following patrons:

Anonymous (x2)
Angela Bonazinga & Catherine Lewis
Gary & Gwen Conners
The Chris Dahl & Ruth Rowse Charitable Fund
Carol Godsave, *in honor of Bayard Godsave*
Margaret Heminway
Grant Holcomb
Kathleen C. Holcombe
Nora A. Jones
Kathy & Mark Kuipers
Paul LaFerriere & Dorrie Parini
Jack & Gail Langerak
Joe McElveney
Boo Poulin
Deborah Ronnen
David W. Ryon
Elizabeth Spenst
Sue S. Stewart, *in memory of Steven L. Raymond*
William Waddel & Linda Rubel
Michael Waters & Mihaela Moscaliuc